MOMENTS OF THOUGHT

Dr Sriya Gunasekera

MINERVA PRESS

LONDON
MONTREUX   LOS ANGELES   SYDNEY

ISBN 1 86106 804 2

First Published 1997 by
MINERVA PRESS
195 Knightsbridge
London SW7 1RE

Printed and bound in Great Britain by
Antony Rowe Ltd, Chippenham, Wiltshire

MOMENTS OF THOUGHT

Dedicated to my brothers and sisters

Drawings by Dr Shahen Tamrazians

Acknowledgement

Special thanks to Mr Lennard Harry
and Dr Shahen Tamrazians

Contents

The Birth of Spring

It is the morning of first day of Spring this year
The happy tunes and chitter-chatter of birds I can hear
The sun is streaming through in front to my patchy green
The brown leaves of Winter in the hedge got a golden sheen

The huge trunks of trees beyond are lit up by the sun
Branches making moving patterns on the trunks have their fun
They do this by hindering the sunbeams as they traverse their
    way
The birds twitter and flit across the boughs to say, today is our
    day

Beyond the spreading lawn, the dancing shadows and the
    chestnut trees
Is a copper beech tree with loveliest pink blossoms one ever
    sees
A host of crocuses have sprung at the foot of the oak with
    message of Spring
Ere other trees and plants had notice and let their buds still to
    hide and cling

The Winter scenes I loved to watch will in no time change
Welcome Spring! and look forward to your colourful range
Goodbye to the nude trees showing their lovely forms with no
    grooms
Memory carries to Spring the shapes under the buds and the
    blooms.

Scenes From a Hillside

On this wonderful dawn in early May
The dark grey spreading mountain yonder lay
With a cliff and a trough and a node and a peak
All across the horizon, looking so sleek

Below the clear blue sky over the range
Varying colours, blue, black to orange
Light up an elongated band of cloud
Giving the mountain a beautiful shroud

Thirty-something degrees above, to left extreme
With no other stars or moon on the sky's scene
In the clear blue sky shines Venus so bright
Alone and supreme, it is a wonderful sight

Now the scene before me changes slow
At the mountain foot, sea appears in the morning glow
Clouds change colour and yellows brightening
Feathery strands along the borders upward spreading

As the black of the night gives way to seeping light
Venus's glory fades and ceases to be so bright
She gets smaller and dims as day chases the night
And giving way to approaching sun, disappears from sight

Now the sleeping town is waking to the fresh of day
A few vehicles I discern, down below on the highway
At the end of this lane with the dawn I can see
A man starts watering his plants and flowering tree

The houses and shops show up clear and pleasing
There run the yellow trains the earliest this morning
One goes to Wallsbaay and another to Cape Town
Beyond the highway, behind the houses, up and down

While I forget the rest of the world on my holiday seated here
In this veranda, enjoying the changing scenes both far and
    near
My children have been quiet in their rooms fast asleep
My beloved friend and her husband too in slumber deep.

Stanmore

Cars, cars, cars
All stationary.
A car park!
Beyond is a row of green trees
Then houses, houses, houses
I see the roofs
Brick-red roofs
With chimneys on all.
Between the houses are other trees
White, brown, and pink
Far away the land rises
A footpath I see
A lady walks up the slope
Dressed so gay
Makes a lovely sight.
Seated in the tube
As I look out
The scenery pleases me
I don't mind the delay.

Wintry Morn

This early winter's morn
five a.m. and yet to dawn
Two weeks more to birth of spring
I open the window wide
and look at the outside

It is dark outside as inside
The huge chestnut trees stand beside
my lawn, full thirty metres away
leafless, against the sky's white grey

Now I hear the wind bellow
beyond the trees in the distant vale
with the force of a coming gale.

The farther highway comes into view
with a myriad lights
in linear array
They gleam above the darkness
with a clarity in their sharpness
separating the grey white sky
from the pitch-black dark
stretching below

I hear the incessant blowing
of the restless wind
It is dark all around me
The lightness of the sky I see
The gusty wind has reached my home
Suddenly the cable across the lawn
flips up and down

The wind hits my body
and seems to touch my soul
cool, refreshing, and soothing
against the central heating
that enfolded me the night

The contrasts of the warmth and the cold
the grey of the sky, and the black of the night
the cries of the winds as they wheeze
the stillness of the trees
bring me a feeling as they combine
exquisite, peaceful, and divine.

Respite

The days gone by have been depressing
Children fighting, and with my life they were messing
Was thinking of life's cares and worries
They seemed to take the joy out of living
Life did not seem worth the living

But now as I sit here crouched, in my towelling robe
And glance up at this minute fraction of the globe
I see the far static clouds lit up and glow
The nearer thin woolly ones moving slow
The leafless plane trees motionless and sunlit
Now the terminal branches moving bit by bit
As the twigs get gently wafted in the wind
Peace comes stealing and embraces my restless mind

I see the rooftops, trees, the tower and the sky
A cosy little birdie sits on a twig, too cosy to fly
Into oblivion have flown away my cares and worries
As I behold the glory of what I see
The joy of living has returned to me
And life seems to be worth the living.

Young Love

Come my love, and sit by my side
Let your tiny fingers to mine slide
As our fingers in love entwine
We know the world is yours and mine

Let us not think of the past or future
We must this dear present nurture
Our love is for now and eternity
We have no doubts, only certainty

We now shall stop the passage of time
Let your watch stop, I threw away mine
The wonder of these minutes or hours
Will forever dwell in these hearts of ours.

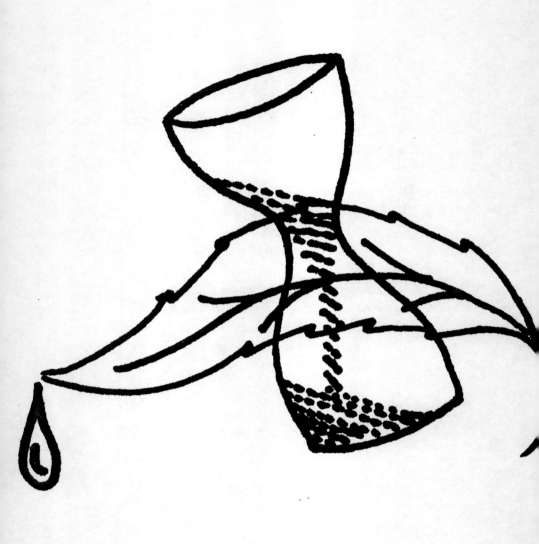

On Your Birthday

It is your eightieth birthday morn
My thoughts go flying your way
Times happy and sweet come reborn
To mine memory so warm and so gay

Many years have passed
Memories fresh as a dawn's dew
The evenings we spent together
Come dancing to my mind's view

The little pearls of wisdom
You strewed before me
The tales of long ago
That entranced me

The sweet nothings uttered
Hours passed not knowing
Passage of time little mattered
For the hours were glowing

So my dear friend, so far away
Thinking of you I make a wish
For me, that future brings my way
Many such evenings with you

And for you, many happy returns
With much love on this special day
And long life and joy in days to come
With health and happiness all your way!

Parting

Shall we sit here and talk a while
Do not run away but sit and smile
There is no need to speak if there is nothing to say
You know as I know, this is parting of our way

The history, the physics, the chemistry, it may not be,
I know as you know, I need you and you need me
Beyond gender, beyond love, and beyond reason
To all accepted norms our souls a treason

I fight, you fight, why not knowing
For certain defeat looms ahead aglowing
The system, the others, the world grins
As I falter we know there are no wins

When I fall I want to get up again
But you slither away, dither away, in rage with no gain
Do you know you leave a shoreless sad sea
To swim or sink in, for a helpless me?

Now we know there is nothing to be done anymore
I know you are hurt, tired, and very sore
Well, go you your way but one more tender smile
For the soul to cherish as she weeps all her while.

The Estranged Wife

She was the estranged wife
Alienated in the winter of her life
Several decades of connubial strife
Ended in two carefree words she uttered
Meant to keep the family unity unshattered

A terrible battle over the trivial remark
He showered her with shit and filth so stark
He called her 'you woman', as the final result
And thought he did the ultimate insult
Then decided to cut her out of his life

She had done so much so long, uncomplaining
For the intolerant, the ungrateful and the unwilling
Tolerating, and grateful for the very little
Till age had its toll, and bones turned brittle
And frail, as mother nature deemed it to be

She turned her back to the dream she had shaped
For it ended in a nightmare that gaped
She kicked her past and her childhood dream
Stood demanding her rightful place in the cosmic scheme
And with a mind as fresh as the morning dew
She started walking towards the stars.

Discussion and Repercussion

Bestiality when the princess met the lion
Human male and female were their scion
Incest when the sibs cohabited with each other
Patricide when the son aimed an arrow at the father

He became king and his son was an impossible kid
He banished him and his chums with shaven head
They floated and landed on a copper-coloured portion
Of the pearl-shaped island in the Indian Ocean

He met the powerful Kuveni plying her loom
She little knew the prince would bring her doom
And some day let her down, she had no notion
When she forsook her kith and kin in her emotion

Was there love, or only guile when he espoused her
She bore their children, a son and a daughter
Then he wanted a foreign princess to wed
And Kuveni with the children to the jungles fled

The jungles echoed her heart-broken wailing
The fatherless children followed, moaning and weeping
The story goes further to describe their plight, saying
The pathetic voices are still in the jungle winds assailing

In His all-pervading kindness to all the beings
The Buddha foresaw the beautiful island's future scenes
He visited the land no less than times three
To help the people from mire rise and be vile-free

But genes after generations can still breed true
For when a little girl was no more than years three
The paedophiles of the land had their way
No wonder! when you know what the stories say

My friend happens to see the story of the race I rhymed
And condemns me for writing a history of this kind,
"People do not run down their own, be it war or lechery
Every race's past has tales of vile deeds and treachery

The princess did not cohabit with a lion
It is not possible, and could not have been so
It was only a man by the name of Lion
And sister and brother married in a custom of yore

Patricide has occurred in the history of many a nation
You better read Freud to know of father and son
The prince got a queen from beyond the ocean
Such things can happen with any royalty under the sun

Little girls are sexually abused all over the world
By dirty men who want to have their vicious fun
It's not a strange or uncommon fact for one to be told
You cannot condemn a nation for what is everywhere done."

By my friend's talk I stand shocked and confused
Can the disgust felt towards one's own people
Be transferred to men all over the world
To be diluted and diffused?

Rolling Stone

Let me be a rolling stone
I have no wish to gather moss
As it rolls in the flowing waters
Let it shape and get a gloss

One may say I am no patriot
But I think of earth as my home
Nature and humans matter
Not the spot where I was born

No desire for permanent roots
If soil's right they sprout anywhere
When the surroundings hamper me
I have to transplant elsewhere

Variety is the spice of life
Places have their special fare
Nature has many a pleasant surprise
And wonderful people live everywhere

Do I miss the loved ones left behind
But with the phone, the fax and the net
The transport, the trains and the aeroplanes
The earth does each day smaller get

My dear friend who lives
A good six thousand miles away
Said unto me do not fear
We are but a thought's distance away

Have trekked to far away places
Some things do remain the same
The sky and the sea you don't have to miss
And the sun and the moon shine the same

So why not be a rolling stone
And roam from where you were born
There is many a green pasture
With the sun and the moon and the corn.

Silence

What the lips do not say
The eyes may
What the eyes cannot say
The body can
The sign language
The body language
What the lips, eyes and body cannot say
The mind may
Telepathy, empathy
Can the soul communicate?
I do not know
But between us there is only silence
Steel cold silence
So close, yet so far.

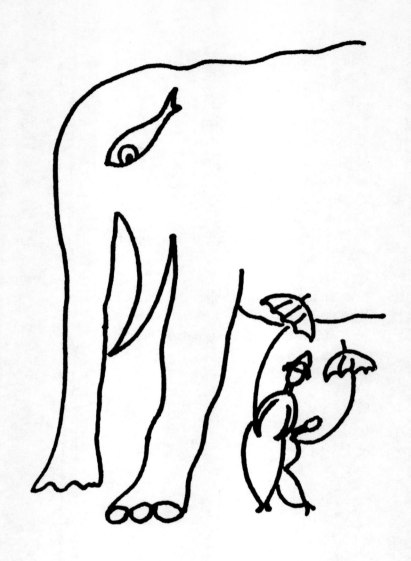

Elephant in the Drawing Room

We go on as if everything is fine
Everyone apparently towing the line
But all the time there is impending doom
It is the elephant in my drawing room

No one talks of the creature hovering there
I don't know if others see or care
It's intruding into space; morning, night and noon
There is an elephant in the drawing room

I am aware of it all my day
And in the night, in my bed as I lay
It spreads a pervading, silent gloom
An elephant lives in my drawing room

No outsider who comes and goes
Sees the big lump as it floats
Inmates remark about the garden in bloom
Not a word of the elephant in the drawing room

Now I am determined to find a way
Of getting the animal out one day
My plan should make it quite very soon
Oh elephant! leave my drawing room.

The Trance

Back to my flat for another week's work
After a weekend with family and home
Away from those near, dear, and mine
Let me sit a while and refresh my mind
Before I walk to the wards
Passing the great oak trees.
Fixed gets my concentration as I watch
Breath hold sway, and air the nostrils touch
Then suddenly I see no more
No care, no worry, no body, no mind
Sans time, *sans* space, *sans* you, *sans* me!
Then up for my walk
Passing the lovely trees
To work.

Home and the Hurt

Home is where the hurt is
Home is where the bond is
Mind is where the hurt lurks
And with it the heart irks

Home is where the hurt is
Home is where the love is
Bonds can lead to breaks
And a mind go to shakes

Home is where the hurt is
Home is where the spouse is
Power to hurt and sadness creeps
Mind then silently weeps

Home is where the hurt is
Home is where the progeny is
Bonds stretch and sanity wanes
Love brings little gains

Home is where the hurt is
Though it's also where the joy is
Home has its compensations
In spite of the irritations

If you accept the joy
Be ready for the hurt
The greater the love
The worse the hurt

But if the hurt becomes too much
You don't have to go on as such
If you don't want the hurt to bear
Learn to let go and have no share!

Our Father

An only child was born eighth of June
His mother said, "Among stars a moon"
He fathered you and me
Full dozen sibs had we
We were the stars and he the moon

Our provider, teacher, and ally
To you, to me, and the many
Steady rock to lean on
Bright beacon to guide on
We loved him and did not tarry

We did not see a brighter moon
In our firmament he was the boon
He lit our childhood days
In youth he scented our ways
Harder than steel, yet gentle as the moon

He never failed one or the other
He had a helping hand to offer
Generous to the extreme
To all he gave the cream
We recall with love and respect! Our father!

Parting Partners

It looks like parting of our ways
After two years and a few more days
Now I am convinced that's what you seek
I will not be an obstacle and will be meek

When I walked with you as your partner
I looked only at the good and needed no pardoner
Always blind to the bad and grateful to the good
Making our way pleasant over highway or wood

You had a lot of good that made me glad
So did you have some things, I think were bad
To make the parting easy, and not make me sad
Let me keep my mind only on the bad

Your ego was one of extreme
Thought you were the life's cream
And should be everyone's dream
You despised what I thought supreme
I think that was bad

You were kindly but love was always lacking
I valued friendly sharing and affectionate caring
You did not approve many things I did and said
Unaware of the good that providence before you laid
I think that was bad

To some you were the icon of masculine cool
The cool could thaw and reason loose its rule
In anger you could raise your voice
Drive away peace and I had no choice
I think that was bad

You thought you were always right
And caused on some relationships a blight
You never bothered how others felt
And they felt hurt and unfairly dealt
I think that was bad

So good luck and farewell!

Tomorrow

Does the night love the moon
Does the sun love the noon
I do not know if they do
But my love is only for you
Do you love me?

Dark goes with the night
With the day the light
The world has much to show
I want to places go
Will you come with me?

The girl walks with the boy
The child hugs her toy
Mother carries her baby
They all look so cosy
Will you be with me?

Even if you do not love me
I will always love thee
If you will not come with me
I will not cross the sea
If you will not be with me
I will be with none.

Let me answer you here and now
Love like that deserves my love
If you want to many places go
To you I will not say no
I will always be with you
You will be the only one

But will you want me tomorrow
As you want me today
What will happen when I am old
Feeble and not so bold
And not able to places go?

Will you continue to care
And with your love dare
When my hair has turned to white
Wrinkles on my face a sight
Will your love sustain?

Will you still need me
When life's cares irk me
And turn me sad
Mood not always glad
No longer bright and young?

Will you want to be with me
When unkempt and sickly
Children leave us when grown
And when I am dead and gone
Will there be a daisy a day for me?

The Change

Who would think, seeing us yesterday
That world would change for us today?
Who would think, seeing us this morn
That world would change for us this noon?
The impermanence

After many years of communication
After the unity and the consolidation
With a few minutes of challenging voice
You decided to be mute by choice
When I spoke to you

Living our normal life yesterday
We could never dream this change today
This morning there was no prelude or ring
To the disaster the later day would bring
To our relationship

It must certainly be our destiny
Was it not destiny that brought you to me
Your voice that seemed to come from far away
Turned my eyes, and the voice had its day
Destiny's trick

You made the decision, it was now enough
To me it sounded extremely rough
You wanted only like this, no other way
I gave you my reasons, I had my say
Though to deaf ears

It did not appear so serious at the time
I thought it immaturity, and no crime
Humbled and amused, I saw me on my knees
But for our tomorrow you grasped the keys
It takes two to tango

Everything is subject to change
Constant is the flux over the range
I knew of impermanence only too well
But knowledge takes long to make it sell
Stand convinced!

Perhaps it is best it happened this way
As our ends must be nearing the day
It would lessen the pain of losing the other
As faith and dependence we will have neither
Destiny wills!

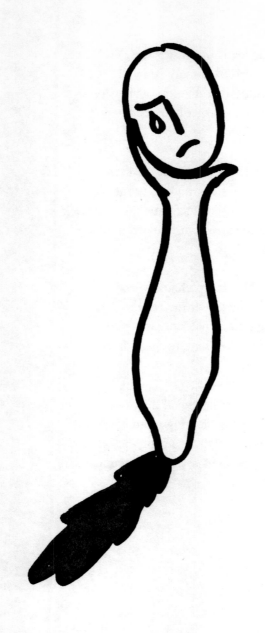

I Wept Today

Today I wept for a little girl
Who lived long ago,
I am not used to weeping for anything
But today I let myself go

She was humiliated and punished
For no wrong of her own
By the head teacher of her school
For something done by the grown

I don't know how she felt
The tumult in her growing brain
She stood on the step of the door
When on her shoulder came the cane

Did she writhe in pain
Or keep her lips tightly shut?
How did the little heart pulsate
When on her fell the unkindly cut?

There is no knowing what she suffered
She was too little to have any say
I imagined her innocent sweet face
And wept in pain, for that day.

Time Will Tell

The girl was perfect
In every respect
Our gem, our pearl

Sweet smile
With no guile
Honey in her gentle words

So very coy
Constant joy
So dear to our hearts

She took to her wings
We helped her whims
Back to us fully grown

No longer coy
There is no joy
The woman's a puzzle

Leaves our hearts broken
Many a word spoken
With hate and guile

Where has the sweetness gone
The love and kindness flown?
We understand her no more

Will the charm ever return
Our sadness to joy turn?
We wait for time to tell.

Childhood Days

Far, far away in a distant rural village
She spent her childhood till ten her age
Children played catches between coconut trees
With rounded pebbles and shells, games to please

The fields of paddy green, then gold
The harvest with corn and hay to mould
The sprouted seeds splayed, then the transplanting
All these occasions the villages celebrating

The kids had a wonderful time on festival day
They played hide and seek on mounds of hay
Food taken to fields was special and mouth-watering
The fragrance of the fare beyond describing
And spread over village giving olfactory relief
Food was served to one and all on plantain leaf

She went to school passing a rubber land
And the raised paths on the paddy fields and the sand
Then walked over two logs laid across the stream
And watched the fish below in crystal-clear water gleam

There was no dearth of fruits in the garden flourishing
Dozens of banana types in various flavours thriving
Available with no break, all year through
It was a haven for children and adults too

There was a large sprawling cashew grove
With low branches parallel to ground and strong did prove
Kids sat on them, walked on them, and they clung
They plucked the nut with the berry as they swung
Ate the berry, yellow, orange, or red, they knew when ripe
Gathered the nuts and took them for the servants to cleave
Never dared to open them because of the corrosive glue
The nut had a wonderful milky taste when fresh
Cooked too it made a festive delicacy dish

Her grandfather was a high-caste, grand, wonderfully gentle
    man
Loved and respected by all except the one named the Froggy
    man
When grandpa was ill and going to hospital on his dying day
The Froggy is supposed to have tried to block the car on its
    way

A finer lady than the grandma she had not seen in the village
    creed
Every night she would sit at the round table and loudly read
She knew many interesting tales which to children's delight
    she related
By heart she knew all native poetry, and other verses too she
    recited

The father was scarcely at home during the day
With some Western education he was employed away
The mother was the gentlest lady one could have known
She wore a long skirt and the tops had lace and cut-work lawn
The doors and windows adorned by her crocheted curtains
And she was adept at making beautiful paper flowers
None of her children learnt her arts of crochet or her flowers

She also knew the local herbs and leaves, and the art that
    healed
Learnt from her father, a native physician, before she married
She grew her own herbarium in the spacious garden
Whenever villages wanted help, there was no delay to pardon
She never raised her voice in anger, or seen to be sullen
Villages pronounced that she was a Path Winner, in local
    jargon

When the child was mischievous and romped about
"We spoil her too much," the grandma did shout
"After all, it's not as if we will give her in marriage
To a doctor or an advocate when she comes of age."
Strange to say the girl became a doctor and married an
    advocate
When the grandma in her ripe old age died
She had her doctor granddaughter by her side
In the city's expensive nursing home
It was also she who cared and looked after the Froggy's
    daughter
When she came at death's door to her ward where she was
    doctor

There was a very old man with a very pleasant face
Who often visited grandpa in evenings and chatted for long
He always carried a walking stick to help him along
It was known he had three wives, and each a home
And his posterity spread wide over the village dome

The house also had a stream of other folk visiting
They chatted, helped and never had a meal missing
There were some women and girls with much devotion
Who bring nostalgic memories and glad emotion

She remembers her childhood of village days
Happy memories mingle with some woeful ways
The vegetation so good and the grass always green
Under the grass she saw the snake, by others unseen.

Swear Words

Swear words I do not like
Never used one in my life
They appear to help people in distress
Get over anger, fear and stress
Then they serve a purpose
But I do not like them
I listen with calm and show no emotion
But inside me I feel commotion
Each time I hear a swear word used
Something within me seems abused
It was so when I was a child
When adult too the recoil as wild
So far I have not got immune
Do avoid them with me to commune.

The Classic Progression

The frog became the prince handsome
He was brilliant and no longer loathsome
The princess fell in love at a glance
And the prince loved her and took no chance
He kissed her and promised love eternal
She was delighted, and sought consent paternal
Parental kings and queens bestowed their blessing
Soon they had a carnival-like wedding
And lived happily ever after

Did the 'ever after' last very long?
You must not make such queries, my dear
These things are not crystal clear
Let us not go into all the details
Lest to delight, the tale of frog prince fails.

The Heart and the Head

The heart had no say
The head was the boss
I forgive my heart
Please forgive my head

I know I did seem hard
Though the heart was soft as lard
Your hard heart retaliated
And I was devastated.

Frustration

Each time, loving, waiting
For softness, warmth and trust
Each time rock hard it hits
No shame, only pain
Again waiting
No shame, no pain, still loving

They say silence is gold
But here it cannot hold
Love says she be told
Don't mean to hassle
But ends in a tussle
Hey Love! there is no escape

Trying to fathom the unfathomable
Predict the unpredictable
Solve the insoluble
Struggling on many days
With her mysterious ways
The indefatigable mind.

Robed

Enwrapped in those loose sheets of yellow ochre
With one shoulder so pale and so bare
You look a monk of the holy order
And fill me with awe and respect as I stare.

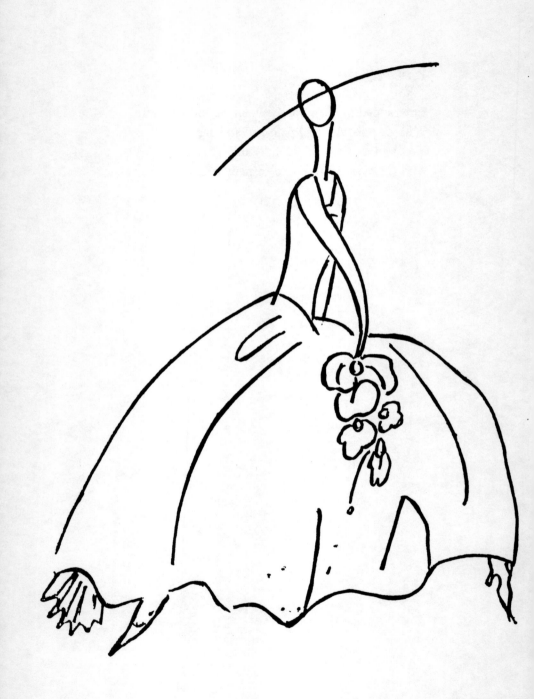

The General's Daughter

People said she was spoiled
And the general's blood boiled
How could there be spoiling
With genes and air not ailing?

Arrogant and eccentric
No doubt elegant and chic
Thoughts and ideas impenetrable
What she does, unpredictable

Can be bright as a button
Kind and loving as a kitten
Then a tigress let loose
Run away to escape her noose

Calm and friendly to the extreme
Then volatile and awkward to deem
What can one do, what can one say?
Close your ears and walk away.

Adieu

Memory does not fade
The eyes a-shine
I remember the sweetness
And smile in my heart
Amidst the work and stress of time
Anxious hours
Striving and the strain
Memory evokes that parting
And taste the sweet serenity
Again and again.
Memory drifts tenderly
A peck on the forehead
No lingering hug
I was on my way
Never to forget
The glow of innocence
As the gentle eyes gazed at me
The angel haunted air
Treasured in memory
Soft and tender, warm and kind
Indelible in the mind.

Adolescence

If you ask a question
There is no reply
A question returns
Instead
It's meant to say
You must not ask
Such questions
It's silly
If you make a comment
Retaliation returns
It need not be so
It's foolish
So it's best to be silent
Lest you want to be
Demeaned and
Confused.

The Cancer

Planned a collection of
preserved flower petals
I plucked a rosebud
Dear little rosebud
As I open your petals
little black creatures
eating into your heart
Thus ending both
a joyful bloom
and eternal life
in my craft.

Paternity

Slave girl Mera lived in a distant village
Wasn't what happened rather savage
She was twelve and with child
Asked who did the action wild
Both the master and his father of old age.

The Delusion

A woman who loved her mother, believed by rebirth
Her dead mother was born her child this birth
Child grew up and one day told her
You are dust and dirt and no other
And the delusion fled forever, to everyone's mirth.

I Screamed

I walked to my door
A slimy lump creeping slow
The slug and my scream!

Suicide

Michelle
Opened window
It was in the fifth floor
She felt death was knocking at her door
She jumped.

Love and Hate

Much love and much hate
Constantly they went up and down
Hate blocked the couple's love
Tears and fears, and laugh and frown
Will love some day hatred win?

Pyramid

I
am
not
gone
madly
insane
lunatic
endanger
ourselves
yourselves
generations
grandmothers
pyramidically
questionnaires
psychopathology
characterisations
schizophrenogenic

My Girl

There lived a mother by the name of Lilly
Her daughter was dear to her and not very silly
Father wanted the girl to marry
Mother said don't to the altar her carry
No man, she said, was good enough for her filly.

Male Depressive Syndrome

I get this burnt-out empty feeling
At times the mind goes reeling
The threshold for tolerance has ebbed low
Frustration creeps at mind's door
I seem to act on every impulse
I cannot help it and up goes my pulse
Irritated by everything around me
Aggressive thoughts consume me
Peers say I have become workaholic
Isn't it better than being alcoholic?
At times I feel like taking some dope
To help me with sadness cope
My wife to the doctor did me drag
He wanted to give me Prozac
Called it the male depressive syndrome
I nearly hit him on his dome!

Modern Time

As a sacred unit my own, my home, me and mine
I used to think of the family, once upon a time
My constant efforts went towards its welfare
And for nothing else so much did I care

Now I realise there is no 'my home or mine'
Members wish not to tow a family line
The flock has their own paths to tread
Family is an impediment they like to shed

Everyone finds family ideas antiquated
Obsolete needing to be liquidated
Modern outlook with no place for give and take
Family unit traditions it wants to break

Each member has a separate way of life
Absolved of family involvements and its strife
About family unity, no one seems to care
In its running they want no share

Today when thinking of home and mine
As I used to once upon a time
It dawned on me the idea was a joke
In the family wheel stands many a spoke

Is this the way with the modern time
There is no more, my home, me and mine
The new thinking trends, to me a mystery
The family as I know it, is history.

Distant Days

We had not seen many another place
Surpassing ours in beauty and in grace
There was no dearth of laughter and fun
We enjoyed the lanes, the trees and the sun.

Pleasant evenings filled with mirth
Friendly chatter of endless girth
Our views in oil, on canvas we shaped
As innovated recipes cooked and baked.

Looking down from where we dwelt
A multitude of lanes over the planes swept
As serpentine and graceful as lanes could ever be
With the distant mansion, delightful to see.

The oaks stood stately as we stared
Against any changing sky full well they faired
Eyes never beheld a scene dull or sour
When views changed with weather, day or hour.

A tough day's work, and some hurtful ways
Did touch our sensitive minds on some days
To heal our wounded spirits and minds to please
We returned to the winding lanes and lovely trees.

Memories

Can you remember the good old days
When we were green little girls in piggy-tails
Mates in class, gentle friends and worthy pupils too
Were not our skies then for ever blue?

In a house by the temple you did abide
With father, mother, sister by your side
There I visited you many a time
Brief were the hours, but the times were fine.

The girls to youth turned
The bonds of childhood endured
They grew stronger as years passed
And all other friendships surpassed.

Life changed, and elders died
Our new families formed and plied
But time brought us closer every day
In sweet friendship.

World seemed to stand still
As catastrophe struck our little isle
Our lives fell apart with seas to divide
And clocks tick, months pass, years ride.

Now as I sit here and ponder
My thoughts fly to you yonder
I think of the half-century just gone
On this early August morn.

Can trust and faith still stand strong
Against such space, time and human wrong?
Did the bonds firm and in gold etched
Snap as beyond endurance stretched?

Yet the fears, chaos, and failures have no feet
As memories stand above and smell! Oh so sweet!

Central Line

"Thank you for travelling by Central Line
This train terminates at Hainault via Newbury Park,"
So says the female voice so fine
It comes daily sweet as the song of a lark

It's the same voice every day
Making the Central Line rather gay
Very pleasing her tone to my ear
Wonder if others feel same as they hear

At times it is found to be very amusing
When leaving says "Change here for Jubilee Line."
If anyone has to use the information
It should come earlier for any jubilation

Still I take pleasure in the voice
To miss it would not be my choice
Soon I have to stop travelling by this train
But it may ring in my ears the sweet strain.

You and Me

Look for me, wait for me

Or let me know
The date, place and time
I will register in my mind
I will find the place somehow
Be it thousand years from now
At Hell's gate or in Timbuktu
I will find the time for you

Have I not waited
Since dawn of time?
You know I will wait
Till end of time
If you want me to

I feel there is no end to time
The meeting is fixed in our mind
Is this only a lovely dream?
Hope beats eternal in our life stream
In expectation we die and we live

You are the distant melody
Not the mirage in the desert
That entices and vanishes.

We will meet in life's tide
And sing, side by side
Only you and me

I shall wait for endless time
Waiting, hoping, happy

But why fool each other?
For we know
There is no you
And there is no me!

Incongruity

There was a tall and lean lady in Lensley
Her laugh burst, whether angry or friendly
Caught the wrong end of the stick
With spite hit the plastic brick
And she laughed and became ever so giggly.

Life Fulfilled

Hooray! I am fifty-five today
I have finished my life's work
And done all I wanted to do
I am ready to go with no ado

Having a carrier
Was no barrier
Enjoyed every bit
The top I hit

Being a mother
Was no bother
It gave me pleasure
I needed no leisure
The girls could not be sweeter
I could not ask for better
There was no sonny lad
Can't miss what you never had

Husband was a man in public life
No easy task, being a politician's wife
But in him I had a rock to lean on
And a friend I could count on

The combination was not easy
Kept me on my feet very busy
I found it not impossible
And I did it
To my satisfaction
And other's benediction
Now my life is complete
There is no more to do
The grave I must woo

My siblings gave constant joy
Boundless love with no ploy
I had wonderful friends
Standing by me to all ends

I have reached the retirement day
Satisfied with life in every way
Now that a life's work is complete
Any more years must deplete

Death! Please do not linger
No need for life any longer
Work done, and I am ready
I would like to come strong and steady

I will wait for you at home
Chat to friends on the phone
Paint murals on walls
Write poetry on scrolls
Come very quick, make it swift
And take me in your arms very gently

Death Passed Me By

Years have passed the day
I requested death take me away
A song of satisfaction I did sing
ready and willing. It gave me no ring

The wait in peace did not last
Country fell into chaos with disaster vast
It encroached on my home, family and me
In the political turmoil we had to flee

Transported to a distant land
with no home and servants at hand
The family found it difficult to handle
and little troubles made a bundle

I did not panic or loose my heart
From bottom I decided to start
Took up full-time work again
to help the family mirth regain

Changed my work to a new discipline
learnt and trained from a slate clean
My peers were less than half my age
With them I felt one and never sage

Though I started work for monetary gain
to help my displaced family sustain
The work gave me renewed pleasure
and experiences I can always treasure
Pleased at the chance to help the sick again

And in the new land I made a home
Met lovely people. Made friends of my own

I do not regret the second lease of life
mainly as I could help family, as mother and wife
My nurturing did not totally help
to rid the indelible marks the uprootment left

My heart goes out to each in love and pain
seeing the coping strategies not all in vain
No satisfaction to make me want to sing

Today I want no death if it comes in my trail
No welcome, I will fight tooth and nail.

Did You Come?

An evening near two score years past
Comes to memory, strange it did last
I went to be on night duty call
My office apart from rest of all
The surroundings so very peaceful
The hopeful feeling within made me joyful.
At the door, a lovely spreading mango tree
With falling dusk no bird or bee
Serene, calm. Still with no duty call
You promised to visit me before nightfall
Was waiting with expectation in my heart
That unusual strange feeling seems still to last
So vivid in my memory, now embers aflame
But I cannot remember if you came.

Siblings

A female child came to be born
And a male sibling when two years gone
With a silver spoon in their mouth
The family belonged to a religious faith
That believed in cycles of birth
And karmic forces causing rebirth

Astrologers were called to have their say
Charts drawn for each inception day
They forecast a bright future on their birth
The sage smiles and grins in his mirth
To say "These children have come to earth
From heavenly realms of wider girth

The girl when she left the domain above
Invited the boy to follow with sisterly love
He later to earth followed suit
To human race in happy pursuit."

They grew up in parental love and care
Sibling rivalry was never there
Schooled together, further studies too
Same pursuits followed the two

They were good friends in those days
Support to each other in many ways
Even when their lives were parted for long
Remembrances carried over like a song
Help across the seas when problems occur
With filial love, concern and succour

Things changed at a very late stage
As they entered the elderly age
He suddenly changed life and himself
And put old relationships on the shelf
He found a new world with friends and care
Wherein the relatives had no share

Her occasional letters went in bin to rest
Her calls aroused in him no interest
She could never fathom the mystery change
He never realised the hurt's range

If they meet in the heavenly abodes above
In a score years or more or less
When they recognise each other
Perhaps he will say to her
"Why did you drag me to the world below?
I would have preferred to continue as before."
She will smile slowly to herself
Glowing in the memory of good days there
And invite another heavenly soul
To accompany her in another sojourn
In the human sphere below
As her sibling.

Mistakes Happen

When a mistake happens
Please do not say
It's you and not me.
For what does it matter
How it happened
And who spoiled the batter
Between you and me.
It has happened
The damage is done
No one is infallible.

Our University Days

We were the three great friends
Together, same in all our trends
We had a time for study, and a time for play
Our families never stood in our way

Days were beautiful and always bright
We had fun, and joy was our right
Between lectures we met under the spreading tree
All times planned, we were the gleeful three

With dull lectures their feet they shuffled
The fatuous coughing not always muffled
Lecturers not bothered by student pranks
We owed to them our grateful thanks

The garden seat by our tree seemed always free
When for each other's company from lectures we flee
Talked of people, their funny ways in happy chatter
Amused, numerous jokes we did scatter

We always dressed prim and proper
Glittered at parties but never behaved improper
We enjoyed the undergrads seen in escapade
Best was the botany trip we three made

After a year we had to part our ways
Missing the spreading tree and carefree days
Shall we meet one day, leaving being mother and wife
And reminisce in rapture that splendid year of our life!